Very special thanks to Dr. Mark Anders and Dr. William Menke of Columbia University
for explaining many of the mysteries of the universe to me on my visit
to Lamont-Doherty Lab in Palisades, NY

Published in the United States 2013 by
🍎 Blue Apple Books
515 Valley Street, Maplewood, NJ 07040
www.blueapplebooks.com

First Edition
Printed in China 10/13
ISBN: 978-1-60905-252-2

1 3 5 7 9 10 8 6 4 2

Design by Elliot Kreloff

Photo credit: Annika Johansson

A **METEORITE** is,
simply speaking,
a rock that survives
a fiery fall from outer space
and lands on Earth.
This happens thousands
of times a year.
Meteorites fall all over
the place: in the sea, in deserts,
on the plain and in jungles
and forests.
They don't usually fall into
people's yards, but this one
did just that! And it happened
not far from New York City
in a town called
Peekskill, New York.

PEEKSKILL
Meteorite

LOCAL FALL

October 9
1992

PEEKSKILL   NEW YORK

But how did the METEORITE get here— to the museum?

Hundreds of millions of miles from Earth, in deep, dark, cold outer space, there are vast fields of space debris flying around: chunks of ice, pieces of satellites, specks of dust, tiny grains of sand, HUGE rocks called asteroids, and smaller rocks called **METEORS**.*

Most of this debris stays up in space. But this is the story of one rock that didn't.

a **METEOR** that falls on Earth is called a **METEORITE**.

Here in outer space is a

METEOR,

likely a broken-off piece of an asteroid,
flying around and around and around.

A year goes by.

A MILLION years go by.

A BILLION years go by.

Over FOUR BILLION years go by.

And then, on October 9th, 1992—

and no one knows exactly why—

the rock changes course and . . .

...enters Earth's atmosphere over the state of Kentucky.

Here is a DOG, sleeping on a porch,
who is awakened by a loud sound.
She barks at the METEORITE...

HISSSSSSSSSSSSSSSSSSSS.......

ANDREA'S HEALTH FOODS

HARDWARE

SAM'S TACKLE

Fried chicken DINNERS

BLUE GRASS MOTEL ½ mile

as it zoomed toward the Earth.

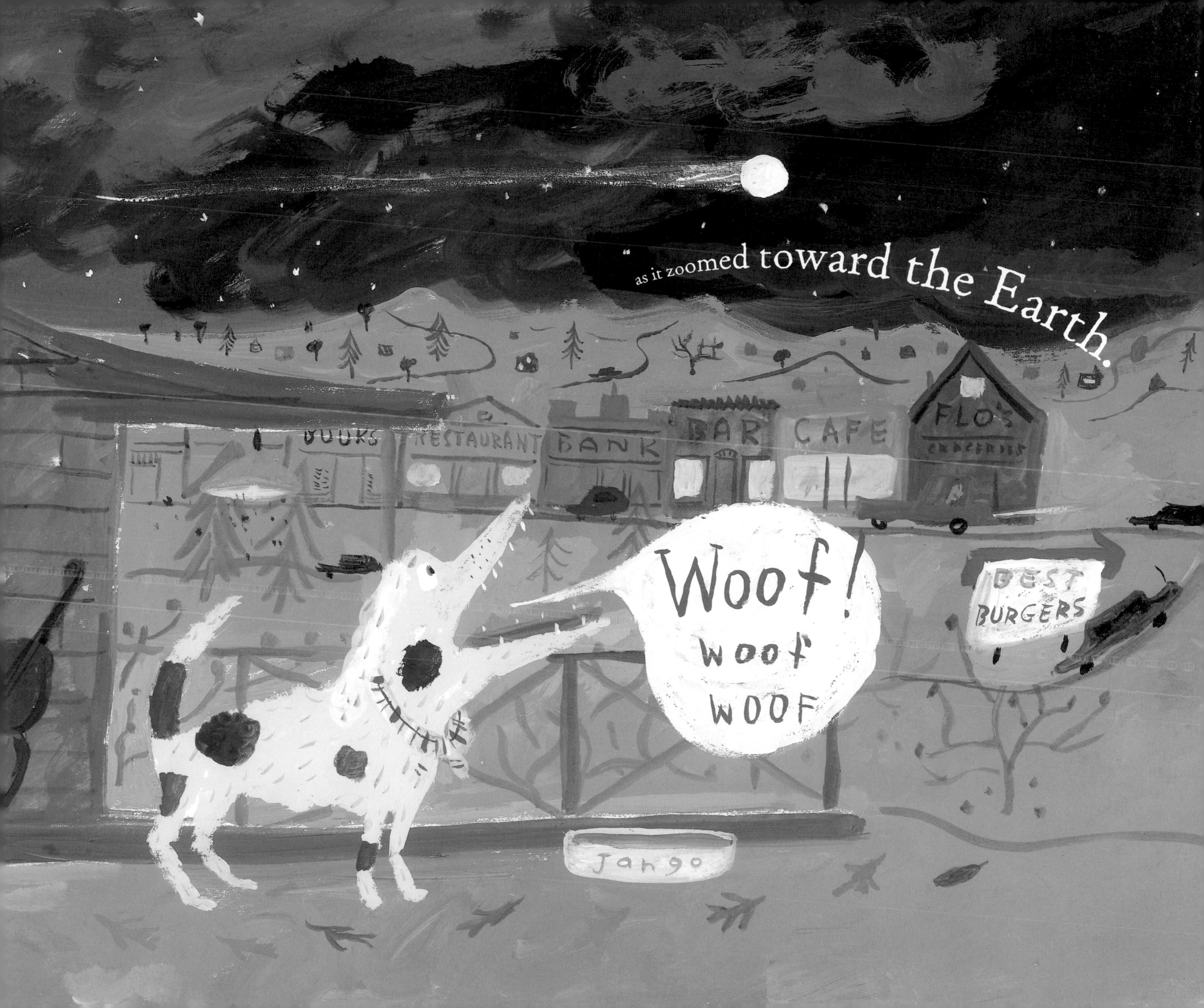

Here are VIRGINIANS enjoying a late-night burger,

who suddenly see a fiery trail in the sky.

We know it was the **METEORITE**, which was . . .

Get a load of that!

BU

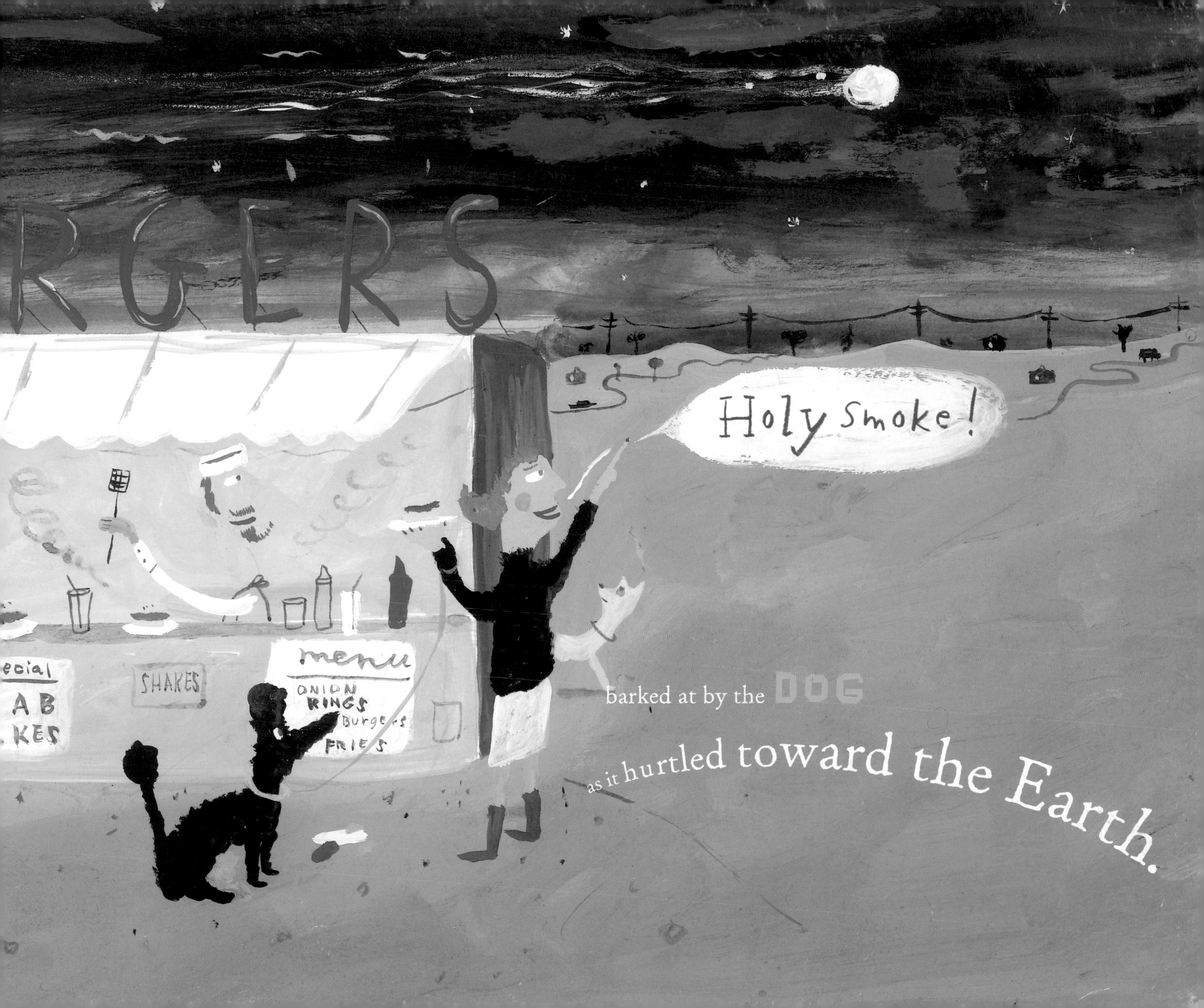

barked at by the DOG

as it hurtled toward the Earth.

Here are **SPORTS FANS** at a Pennsylvania high school football game.

The home team is trailing by 7 . . . the running back has got the ball, 3rd down . . . 4 yards to go!

Home movie cameras point to the action on the field until . . .

ZZZ—**CRACK** HISSSSSSSSSSSSSSSSSSS

More exciting than a flying football is the **METEORITE**, which was . . .

spotted by the VIRGINIANS,

and yelped at by the DOG

as it zipped toward the Earth.

Here is the  **TEENAGER**, who had been watching late-night TV at her house in Peekskill, NY, when she heard a tremendous **CRASSHHH!** She has rushed outside and discovered a huge dent in the trunk of her car and a smoking "rock" nearby. Of course, it is really the **METEORITE**, which was . . .

Who threw this rock?

filmed by **SPORTS FANS**,

pointed at by **VIRGINIANS**,

and woofed at by the **DOG**

as it sped toward the Earth.

Here are the **POLICE**, who rush to the scene.
They poke and prod at the still-warm "rock"
and declare "criminal mischief" for what really was
caused by the **METEORITE**, which was . . .

discovered by the TEENAGER,

recorded by SPORTS FANS,

spotted by VIRGINIANS,

and howled at by the DOG

as it bolted toward the Earth.

Here are the **FIREFIGHTERS**,

called to cool the "rock," which has caused gas—EEK!—

to drip from the car's punctured fuel tank.

They start to suspect that the rock may really be

a **METEORITE**, which was . . .

examined by the **POLICE**,

reported by the **TEENAGER**,

videotaped by **SPORTS FANS**,

pointed at by **VIRGINIANS**,

and ruffed at by the **DOG**

as it plunged toward the Earth.

Here is a GEOLOGIST,

a scientist who studies rocks

to learn about the history of the Earth.

He has come to Peekskill, NY,

from Columbia University to investigate

the mysterious "rock."

He confirms that what smashed the car

is, indeed, a METEORITE,

which was . . .

cooled by **FIREFIGHTERS**,

investigated by **POLICE**,

found by the **TEENAGER**,

gawked at by **SPORTS FANS**,

buzzed about by **VIRGINIANS**,

and arfed at by a **DOG**

as it raced toward the Earth.

Here is the **CURATOR OF METEORITES** from the American Museum of Natural History in New York City. He is admiring the space rock and hoping to obtain at least a slice of it. The museum would love to add to its collection this **METEORITE**, which was . . .

This likely came from an asteroid belt between Jupiter and Mars. The museum would love to add this meteorite to its collection.

GEOLOGY

eon

era   Paleozoi

period

cretaceous

GEOLOGY Dept. Columbia 1964

Cenozoic *

MESOZOIC | Cenozoic

Triassic | Jurassic | Cretaceous | Paleo | Neo

identified by a GEOLOGIST,

cooled by FIREFIGHTERS,

cordoned off by POLICE,

called in by a TEENAGER,

taped by SPORTS FANS,

remarked on by VIRGINIANS,

and arfed at by the DOG

as it crashed toward the Earth.

Here we have an H-6 monomict breccia meteorite with a weight of 26 lbs. The luminous flight time exceeded 40 seconds and covered 400-500 miles—a speed of better than 10 miles per second! Simply put: it's an old rock from outer space that came here fast. The chance of a meteorite colliding with a car is about ONE-IN-A-BILLION!

Here is the **COSMOLOGIST**, a scientist who specializes in outer space, explaining everything you may want to know—AND MORE!—at a museum symposium about the **METEORITE**, which was . . .

METEORITE

procured by the CURATOR OF METEORITES,

confirmed by the GEOLOGIST,

hosed by FIREFIGHTERS,

poked at by POLICE,

called in by the TEENAGER,

chronicled by SPORTS FANS,

whooped at by VIRGINIANS,

and yipped at by the DOG

as it fell toward the Earth.

Here is the **EXHIBITS TEAM**

at the Natural History Museum

designing the lighting, signage and diorama

for their newest acquisition, the soon-to-be-famous

METEORITE, which was . . .

PEEKSKILL METEORITE

PEEKSKILL Meteorite

LOCAL · FALL

october 9 1992

PEEKSKILL NEW YORK

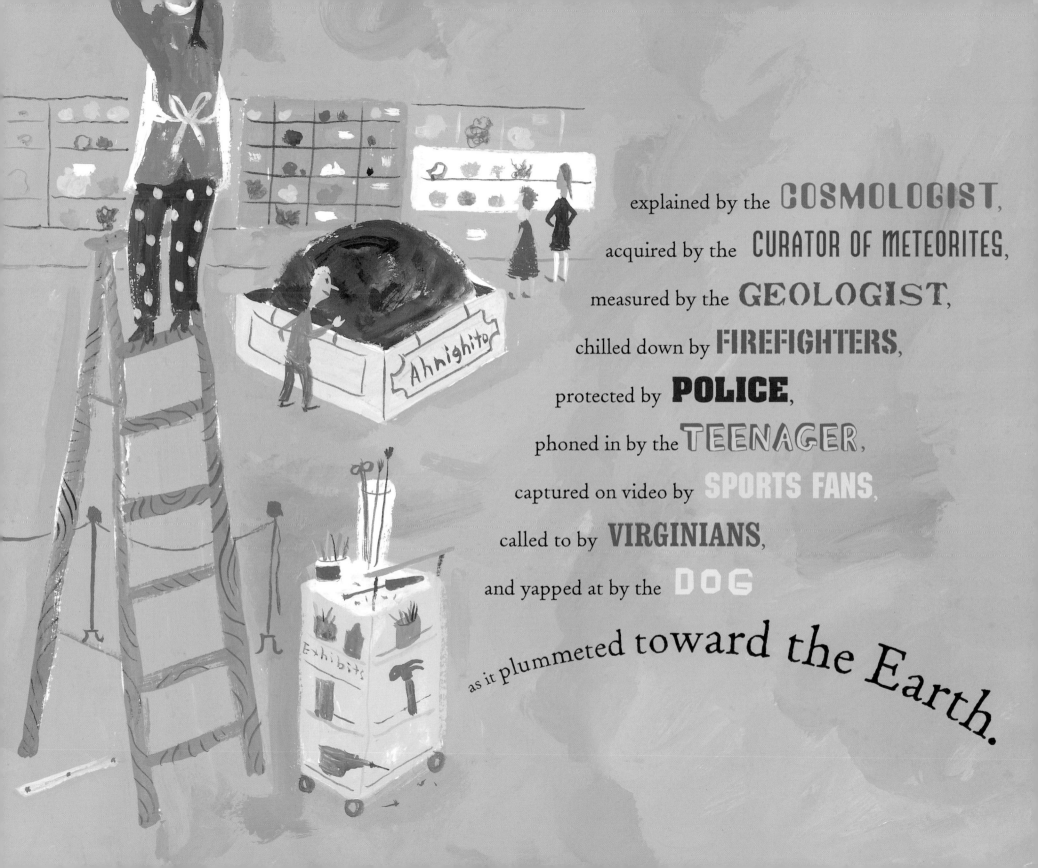

explained by the COSMOLOGIST,

acquired by the CURATOR OF METEORITES,

measured by the GEOLOGIST,

chilled down by FIREFIGHTERS,

protected by POLICE,

phoned in by the TEENAGER,

captured on video by SPORTS FANS,

called to by VIRGINIANS,

and yapped at by the DOG

as it plummeted toward the Earth.

Here is the **SCIENCE TEACHER**, who guides her students through the Ross Hall of Meteorites. She loves the study of the mysteries of outer space and sharing that with her students.

Now surrounded by a crowd of new young fans is the Peekskill **METEORITE**, which was . . .

barked at by the **DOG**,

witnessed by **VIRGINIANS**,

filmed by **SPORTS FANS**,

found by a **TEENAGER**,

poked at by **POLICE**,

sprayed with water by **FIREFIGHTERS**,

validated by the **GEOLOGIST**,

obtained by the **CURATOR OF METEORITES**,

summed up by the **COSMOLOGIST**,

presented by the **EXHIBITS TEAM** and . . .

More About Meteors

The GEOLOGIST who appears in this book is Dr. Mark Anders of Columbia's Lamont-Doherty Lab. He kindly met with the author, Jessie Hartland, and answered many questions.

Dr. Anders first viewed the meteorite at the Peekskill Police Department. Because it had traces of red paint on it, at first he didn't think it had come from outer space. But when he saw where it had landed, and the smashed red car, he changed his mind.

The Peekskill Meteorite, property of teenager Michelle Knapp, was eventually sliced up into pieces and sold for more than $69,000.

The American Museum of Natural History indeed has one of these pieces on display in its Ross Hall of Meteorites. You can go see it for yourself! Chicago's Field Museum also has a slice, as does the Smithsonian; other pieces are in private collections.

The 1980 Chevy Malibu, which survived except for the massive dent, was sold for $10,000. It went on to tour the world. With the money, Ms. Knapp was able to buy a brand-new car.

What caused the Peekskill Meteorite to change its course and collide with Earth? It may have been nudged off its orbit by something as small as a grain of sand. Or perhaps it was a puff of gas emitted from the sun. Whatever the cause, it was a random act of nature.

Dr. Mark Anders demonstrates the meteorite's trajectory through Michelle Knapp's Chevy Malibu.

Most meteors disintegrate as they enter the Earth's atmosphere. Meteors falling during daylight hours are not likely to be noticed.

Roughly 500 meteors actually land on Earth each year, but only five or six are ever seen or found. Many fall in oceans or other uninhabited areas. And most of them look like ordinary rocks.

METEORITES are always named for the place where they land.

In the U.S., meteorites belong to the person upon whose land they are found.

There are three types of meteorites: iron, stone, and an iron/stone mix. The Peekskill Meteorite is a stone meteorite.

If you stand outside on a clear, dark night for about half an hour, chances are you will see at least one meteor streak across the sky.

If you have a fear of being hit by a meteorite, you are a meteorophobe.

Every day, millions of tons of space debris, including METEORITES, fall upon our planet.

Maybe the next famous METEORITE will be called "{your name's} backyard"!